My Grandmother Calls Me

BEAUTY

Written by Erin Johnson and Lakenya Johnson

Illustrated by Emily Hercock

To "Mama Cat" and Mimi

About The Authors

Erin Johnson, a fun and loving first grader, hopes to become a teacher and/or ballerina someday.

When she isn't helping her mom with her two younger brothers, she can be found reading or singing. She hopes to inspire other children to read more, walk in confidence, and tell their story.

Lakenya Johnson is a proud wife, mother, and Speech Therapist.

A Louisiana native, she is a lover of naps, music, and good food.

This Book Belongs To:

My grandmother calls me
Beauty and she gives me great
big hugs.

She tickles me and plays with me
and shows me lots of love.

My grandmother says I'm pretty
and she also says I'm smart.

And times when we are far apart
I keep her in my heart.

Grandma

Sometimes my grandmother reads
with me and gives me yummy treats.

She cooks all of my favorite
things—especially the sweets!

My grandmother can do lots of things,
like once... she hemmed my dress.

And when Mama and Daddy say no,
she ALWAYS tells me yes!

Her house is where I play, have fun and be completely free.

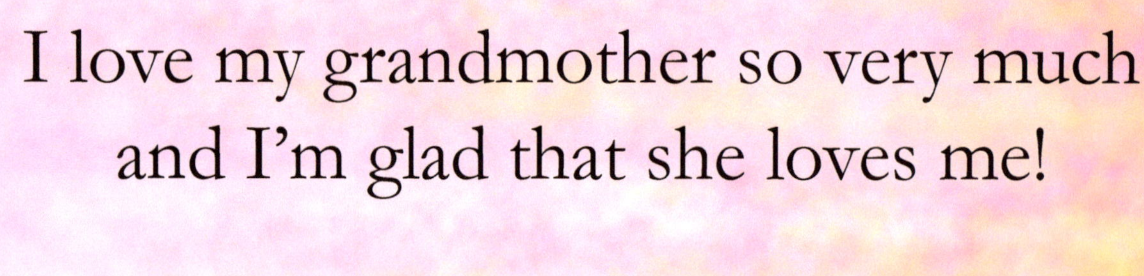
I love my grandmother so very much
and I'm glad that she loves me!